Fact Finders®

PERSPECTIVES on HISTORY

MARIE ANTOINETTE

FASHIONABLE QUEEN OR GREEDY ROYAL?

by Sarah Webb

Raintree is an imprint of Capstone Global Library Limited, a company incorporated in England and Wales having its registered office at 7 Pilgrim Street, London, EC4V 6LB – Registered company number: 6695582

www.raintree.co.uk
myorders@raintree.co.uk

Text © Capstone Global Library Limited 2015
The moral rights of the proprietor have been asserted.

Editorial Credits
Brenda Haugen, editor; Heidi Thompson, designer; Svetlana Zhurkin, media researcher; Laura Manthe, production specialist

ISBN 978 1 406 29302 9 (hardback)
19 18 17 16 15
10 9 8 7 6 5 4 3 2 1

ISBN 978 1 406 29304 3 (paperback)
19 18 17 16 15
10 9 8 7 6 5 4 3 2 1

British Library Cataloguing in Publication Data
A full catalogue record for this book is available from the British Library.

Photo Credits
Alamy: Mary Evans Picture Library, 14; CRIAimages: Jay Robert Nash Collection, cover (middle right), 21; iStockphotos: GeorgiosArt, 23; Newscom/akg-images, 7 (top), 11, 17, 18, 25, 29, Album/Oronoz, 8, Album/Prisma, 27, SIPA/E.R.L, 5; Shutterstock: abadesign, cover (background), Daniela Migliorisi, 13; SuperStock: Fine Art Images, cover (bottom)

Design Elements by Shutterstock

Direct Quotes
p. 9 from *Marie Antoinette: The Journey* by Antonia Fraser (New York: N.A. Talese/Doubleday, 2001)
p. 17 from *Marie Antoinette: The Last Queen of France* by Evelyne Lever (New York: Farrar, Straus, and Giroux, 2000) p. 26 from *Marie Antoinette: The Journey*

Printed and bound in China

CONTENTS

A date with the executioner

Marie Antoinette, the former queen of France, waited in the damp, dark cell of the prison as the sun rose on 16 October 1793. She had not slept at all the night before. Her lady-in-waiting softly greeted her. She helped Marie change into a clean dress. Months in prison had left Marie pale and thin.

The executioner tied Marie's hands behind her back. As the prison guards took her outside, she almost fainted. There was no carriage to meet her. Instead she rode in a common cart like a criminal, facing backwards.

The cart travelled through the crowded streets for more than an hour. Some people insulted and shouted at Marie as she rode by. She did not react.

Finally the cart halted in front of a platform. Above Marie a shiny blade hung between two heavy beams. It was a **guillotine**. In a few moments, she would lose her head.

Who was Marie Antoinette? Some said she was a criminal who deserved to die. Others claimed she was just a victim of politics. But what events led to her death?

guillotine machine for executing people by beheading them

Marie Antoinette faced her death with dignity.

Chapter 1

FORMING AN ALLIANCE

Maria Antonia Josephina Johanna was born
2 November 1755, in Vienna, Austria. Her mother,
Empress Maria Theresa, ruled the Habsburg Empire.
She called her daughter Antonia. The girl grew up
in the royal Hofburg Palace. She led a childhood of
pleasure and wealth. Her tutors tried to help her study,
but they often cut her lessons short. Antonia mostly
liked to play.

Empress Maria had big plans for her daughter.
She wanted an **alliance** with France. Austria and
France had long been enemies. The Empress hoped
a royal marriage would keep peace between the two
countries. By the time Antonia was 13 years old, her
mother had arranged for her to marry the **dauphin** of
France, Louis Auguste. He was the grandson of France's
king. Antonia had to follow her mother's wishes. She
was powerless to decide her own future.

alliance agreement between nations or groups of people to work together

dauphin male next in line to be the king of France; the dauphine is the wife of the dauphin

Antonia (third from left) grew up in a wealthy family.

London ★

Netherlands

Belgium

Paris ★

Versailles ★

France

Switzerland

Vienna ★

Habsburg Empire

Italy

Spain

Antonia married Louis surrounded by the French court and the royal family.

Antonia married Louis Auguste on 16 May 1770, in the Royal Chapel at Versailles, France. She was just 14 years old, and he was only 15 years old. They had met just before the wedding. The French called the young bride Marie Antoinette, or Madame La Dauphine. She never saw her mother or her homeland again.

FACT

When she got married, Antonia had to leave her dog, Mops, behind in Austria. She later arranged for him to join her in France.

A DAUGHTER'S PLACE

Antonia was the 15th of 16 children. Empress Maria Theresa believed her young daughters should do whatever she told them to do. She said, "They are born to obey and must learn to do so in good time".

Many of Empress Theresa's sons and daughters married princes and princesses from other countries. Among them were Spain and Bavaria. It was typical at that time for noble children to have marriages arranged by their parents. The marriages formed alliances. Kingdoms needed alliances to protect their borders from enemies.

As a new dauphine, Marie Antoinette had one job. She had to give birth to a male child. An **heir** would continue the royal family. But the couple did not start a family right away.

Louis Auguste and Marie Antoinette spent a lot of time apart. They were both so young and very different. Louis was terribly shy and timid. Marie was charming and bubbly. She liked to attend late-night masked balls, parties and theatre performances. Louis enjoyed hunting during the day and went to bed early. He loved reading about history, geography and science. His wife preferred to play rather than study. Where she was graceful, he was clumsy. He waddled when he walked, while Marie walked as if she was floating on air.

AN EXPENSIVE WARDROBE

The clothing of an entire French working-class family cost about 30 livres. Wealthy nobles spent an average of 2,000 to 5,000 livres on their clothes. By comparison, Empress Theresa spent 400,000 livres on Marie Antoinette's clothing to prepare for her wedding. The Empress knew her daughter needed dresses made of the finest fabrics. Marie wore a silver brocade wedding gown covered with white diamonds. A livre in Marie Antoinette's day was worth between £12 to £18 today. That means Marie Antoinette travelled to France with clothes valued at around £5 million to £7 million.

Marie played the spinet, an instrument similar to the piano.

heir someone who has been or will be left a title, property or money

Chapter 2

BECOMING QUEEN

The dauphin of France, Louis Auguste, became King Louis XVI on 10 May 1774. At just 19 years old, Marie Antoinette was now the Queen of France. In public, the French people appeared to like the new Queen and King. But in private, people were suspicious of the new Queen. They called her "the Austrian woman". French nobles believed that Marie Antoinette would try to control the King with her Austrian advice.

In truth, Marie had no desire to control the King's politics, but she did enjoy his wealth. As Queen, Marie believed she could behave in whatever way she chose. She spent many evenings playing cards and gambling. She often giggled at important events.

FACT

Marie hated the public life at Versailles. Any commoner could be admitted to the court – and the royal rooms – as long as they were well-dressed. People could watch her get dressed, undressed and eat. Up to 10,000 people a day visited the palace at Versailles.

Marie also spent money **lavishly**. She held two costume balls a week at the royal palace in Versailles. At times there may have been between 2,000 and 4,000 other nobles living with the royal family at the palace. The costume balls were expensive events. It did not help Marie's public image that the King gave her a private palace. It was called Le Petit Trianon.

Le Petit Trianon included several buildings and gardens.

lavish spending or giving more than is necessary

Marie sometimes dressed as a shepherdess at Trianon.

PLAYING AT HER PALACE

At Le Petit Trianon, Marie Antoinette had a fake country village built. It included peasant houses, a farmhouse and a dairy. She used her village for outdoor theatre games. She often played the role of a peasant.

Marie's behaviour at Trianon offended older nobles. They viewed her play as childish. They thought she showed disrespect for the throne. Both nobles and commoners did not like that she could hide in her private palace. The Queen spent her days at Trianon and returned to Versailles at night.

Many people misunderstood Marie. At Versailles she had to follow more rules. She was required to eat with certain people and dress a particular way. At Trianon, Marie had more control. She invited only the people she wished to see. Marie hated the stuffy, strict Versailles palace. She wanted a simpler life away from all the rules of Versailles.

Marie also loved helping children and the poor. A poor boy named Jacques once fell under Marie's carriage. Marie jumped out of the coach to help him. Learning the boy was an orphan, Marie adopted him. Servants brought him up at Versailles. In other instances, Marie asked her husband to be generous with his money and to give it to good causes.

These kind actions went unnoticed. In four years as Queen, Marie had made many enemies. Nobles felt the Queen did not respect the French people and ignored too many rules.

FACT

Mean stories and rumours about Marie were sometimes printed in booklets called *libelles*. Stories in the booklets **exaggerated** her actions. Many people learned about Marie only from these booklets.

exaggerate make something bigger or more important than it really is

Chapter 3

A LAVISH LIFESTYLE

After seven years of marriage, the royal couple still had no children. Gossip about being childless threatened Marie's authority. During this time, the Queen used fashion to establish her power. She ordered the finest silk dresses and outfits. She bought 200 to 300 new outfits each year. She purchased four new pairs of shoes each week. Her clothes took up three rooms at Versailles.

Marie also developed a unique hairstyle called a pouf. This hairstyle included ribbons, flowers, ostrich feathers or scenes. The fancy poufs sometimes reached 90 centimetres (3 feet) in height. One themed hairstyle included artichokes, carrots, radishes and even a head of cabbage. Her pouf became a symbol of reckless spending.

French nobles said hateful things about Marie behind her back. Commoners accused her of spending too much money. People did not think Marie acted like a queen. They thought she was silly and wasteful.

Marie dressed in elaborate gowns and had her hair styled in a pouf.

A musical insult

Nobles sang a song about Marie Antoinette to show how they felt about her:

"Little 20-year-old queen/Since you treat people with no shame/You'll go back from where you came."

Marie wore expensive gowns while many poor people in France were starving.

Marie Antoinette misjudged people. She did not understand how the poor felt about her spending. People wrote about her expensive clothes and parties. Marie often changed dresses three times each day. She usually wore her beautiful gowns just once.

Like other nobles, Marie spent a lot of money. But rules required nobles to live lavishly. She also had no control over the King's politics. By the late 1770s France had already spent a lot of money fighting wars against England in America. But the *libelles* blamed France's money problems on Marie's expensive lifestyle.

A TASTE FOR EQUALITY

During the last half of the 1700s, people read about the Enlightenment philosophy in France. Authors wrote that all people were equal. In 1776 the United States adopted the Declaration of Independence and went to war against the British King. France helped the United States, which won its independence in 1783. French soldiers brought back news about the new American government. Feelings against the French **monarchy** were growing among commoners.

monarchy form of government in which a king or queen is head of state

Chapter 4

MADAME DEFICIT

Between 1774 and 1787 people in France experienced severe hunger. Poor harvests and harsh winters caused wheat shortages, which meant no flour for bread. Food riots broke out. Workers grew restless against the monarchy. People blamed Marie for many of their problems. They called her "Madame **Deficit**". They said she spent money recklessly. But the money she spent was just a small part of the problem. The King spent too much money helping the Americans win their independence. Many people did not know this. The King controlled what the newspapers printed about him and his policies.

FACT

During the unrest, Marie supposedly asked why the people rioted. An aide said it was because of bread shortages, since flour was scarce. Some claimed that Marie replied, "Let them eat cake". However, there is no evidence that she actually made this statement. It did not help Marie's image that a main ingredient in hair powder for her poufs was flour.

deficit loss created when government spends more than it takes in

Meanwhile, Marie Antoinette finally had a son: an heir to the throne. Between 1778 and 1786, Marie gave birth to four children: Marie Therese Charlotte, Louis Joseph, Louis Charles and Sophie Helene Beatrice. *Libelles* still wrote hateful things about Marie. They suggested the King was not the father of her children.

A painting of Marie and three of her children

A 1785 scandal also damaged Marie's reputation. A jealous court noble, Comtesse Lamotte, tricked a **cardinal** into a theft scheme. Lamotte told the cardinal that the Queen wanted an expensive diamond necklace. The cardinal told a jeweller that the Queen would pay for the necklace. The cardinal collected the necklace, but Lamotte's husband fled the country with it. Police put Comtesse Lamotte in prison. A trial found the cardinal not guilty. However, this event forever hurt Marie Antoinette's image. She never wanted the necklace, but French citizens believed the Queen was behind the whole scheme. They believed she was uncaring and would rather spend money on diamonds than help the starving people.

In 1787, after what came to be known as the Diamond Necklace Affair, Marie finally began to reduce her spending. She was tired of all the hurtful things that were written about her. Some French people said that the Queen's love of fashion was proof of her cruel nature. Marie stopped wearing so many poufs and silk dresses. She ordered plain dresses made from cotton. Yet nobles still criticized her choices. They thought cotton dresses made her look like a peasant.

cardinal official of the Roman Catholic Church, next in rank to the pope

Marie could not escape criticism even when she wore less expensive clothes.

Her fashion changes also hurt French workers. After Marie stopped ordering fine dresses, several silk factories were unable to pay their debts. Many people lost their jobs. She also bought cotton fabric from England. As a result, people accused Marie of not supporting the French economy. Workers thought she was blind to their troubles of unemployment and hunger.

The people of France could no longer contain their anger. A mob stormed the Bastille, a prison in Paris, on 14 July 1789. The angry men hoped to find gunpowder. The tide had turned. A **revolution** against the monarchy had begun.

Women later became involved in the uprising, too. Their families were starving. They thought the King and Queen selfishly hid flour and bread at Versailles. On 5 October 1789, a mob of women walked 19 kilometres (12 miles) from Paris to Versailles. They demanded lower food prices from the King. Women stormed the palace and destroyed the Queen's rooms. By 6 October, the women marched back to Paris with the royal family as prisoners. They also carried huge supplies of grain with them. The people thought they could make the King listen to their complaints. They viewed Marie as a monster. They blamed her for their suffering.

revolution violent uprising by the people of a country that changes its system of government

republic a form of government in which the people have the power to elect representatives who manage the government

Parisian peasant women marched to Versailles and took the royal family as prisoners.

The royal family lived under heavy guard in the Tuileries Palace in Paris from 1789 to 1791. They still lived comfortably, but they did not have the same freedom they had before. The King was still technically in charge of the country, but he lost more and more power over time.

It was a dangerous time. The Queen did not believe her husband should give in to the people's demands for equality. She thought that divine rule should be saved at all costs. Both the King and Queen pretended to support the causes of the revolution. But they secretly wrote letters to other countries asking for support. Marie hoped her Austrian homeland would send an army to defeat the revolution.

It had also been a heartbreaking time. The royals had lost their son Louis Joseph on 4 June 1789. It was thought he died of some form of tuberculosis, a disease that often attacks the lungs but may have attacked his spine. Marie later said of that summer, "At the death of my poor little dauphin, the nation hardly seemed to notice".

Commoners took control of the government in late 1789. The next year, the new government put an end to all noble titles. The King became Louis Capet, from his family name.

Guards moved the royal family to the Temple, a Paris prison, in 1792. The new French government tried Louis Capet and found him guilty of **treason**. He was **executed** by guillotine, 21 January 1793.

The King said goodbye to his family before he was executed.

treason crime of betraying one's government
execute put to death

Chapter 5

THE WIDOW CAPET

About nine months after her husband was executed, Marie was living in La Conciergerie, another prison in Paris. Now called the Widow Capet, Marie faced charges including treason. On 15 October 1793, a court found her guilty and sentenced her to death. The sentence would be carried out that very day.

The prison cart rolled to a stop near the guillotine. To the cheers of the Paris crowd, the blade fell quickly. Marie's life had ended. She was 37 years old.

What was the truth of Marie Antoinette's life? Her only job was to have a son. Did she have the authority to help the commoners? Did she make things worse with her lavish lifestyle?

Marie's mother forced her into an arranged marriage. New beliefs about French government arose during this time. People wanted to get rid of the monarchy. The new government accused her of treason. Was she really a criminal who deserved to die? Did the revolution encourage the court to execute her? Or was she just a victim of politics?

rie listened as her death
ntence was read.

GLOSSARY

alliance agreement between nations or groups of people to work together

cardinal official of the Roman Catholic Church, next in rank to the pope

dauphin male next in line to be the king of France; the dauphine is the wife of the dauphin

Declaration of Independence document written in 1776 that declared the United States a free and independent country and says that every US citizen has rights that the government should protect

deficit loss created when government spends more than it takes in

exaggerate make something bigger or more important than it really is

execute put to death

guillotine machine for executing people by beheading them

heir someone who has been or will be left a title, property or money

lavish spending or giving more than is necessary

monarchy form of government in which a king or queen is head of state

republic form of government in which the people have the power to elect representatives who manage the government

revolution violent uprising by the people of a country that changes its system of government

treason crime of betraying one's government

READ MORE

France (Countries Around the World), Mary Colson, (Raintree, 2012)

France (Horrible Histories), Terry Dreary (Scholastic, 2011)

Marie Antoinette (Great Queens), Jane Bingham (Raintree, 2009)

Marie Antoinette, Kathryn Lasky (Scholastic Paperbacks, 2013)

WEBSITES

www.bbc.co.uk/history/historic_figures/louis_xvi.shtml

Find out more about Marie and her husband, King Louis.

www.bbc.co.uk/education/subjects/zk26n39

Follow the links to find out more about the French Revolution.

COMPREHENSION QUESTIONS

1. Booklets from the 1780s called Marie Antoinette the "Queen of Vice". Explain what you think they meant by that. Use details from the text to support your response.

2. How do the chapter titles illustrate Marie Antoinette's life? Use details from the text to support your answer.

3. The Enlightenment philosophy encouraged freedom from a monarchy. The people fought for a republic. A republic is a government where the people have the power to elect representatives to make laws. Do you think Marie Antoinette had to die for a French republic to be created?

INDEX